Pastel gras, Monsieur Picasso

My oil pastel journey

Elena Malec

Contents

Contents

Foreword..4
Oil Pastels as Pure Joy...............................6
Pastel gras, Monsieur Picasso....................8
Copying the Masters................................11
Oil Pastels Techniques.............................15
Portrait..24
Still life..29
Botanicals...33
Landscape...39
Genre paintings.......................................43
Self-portrait...44
Afterword..45

"Every child is an artist. The problem is how to remain an artist once we grow up."

= Picasso.

Foreword

The adage of the liberated human in an advanced society and civilization has been for a long time with us, the day people will be free to self-discovery and development.

The technology of our time made possible that we spent more time without toiling and doing strenuous work. Even if we still have no plenty of free time, we are more aware that the spare time we have should be spent on our development and personal growth.

One form that reaches more and more people than before is making art. We can say that we live a visual art past time mania in which people from all walks of life paint and create artworks. Embracing a form of making art is now common in most worldwide communities on five continents. Still an expensive hobby art making is yet more popular than writing which is rather cheap. One major reason for that is the universal language of art. A more direct contact with the audience and a reduced intellectual level. Another aspect of art making is its therapeutic function both on the producer as well as on the receiver. Art can save lives, and not lastly souls.

The aesthetic human is in fact the superior being that differs from other animals through artistic creation.

Dedicating your time and effort to making art can be the ideal way of de-alienation, by no means. If art can heal, it also can enrich you spiritually. Expressing oneself through art requires the training one is ready to undertake provided there is no obligation for it.

The aesthetic dimension of humans is as old as the species and I should say defines the species. Before being political animals, humans were aesthetic beings and the oldest unearthed art findings as well as cave art are conclusive of this.

Being creative is a human function that art claims its own right in more people than scientific research and intellectual work. One thing that sets art apart from science is the fact that in science two people can come to the same discovery or solution while art is with every artist new and unique has the mark of one's personality.

Another dissimilarity between art and science is that that science operates with partial truth while art bears a perennial message, is not a link in a chain but rather an autonomous piece.

A question to be asked is how art relates to human progress. A simple answer is that art is creativity, and creativity is at the core of progress. Making art as a social endeavor can take us to the road to a sane society of liberated human beings, living healthier and longer lives.

Oil Pastels as Pure Joy

If you are a six-years old or a sixty-years old both age groups are right for oil pastels. There is practically almost nothing to teach but lots to learn and enjoy doing it as your heart dictates. A most versatile medium with easy ways of usage and handling, oil pastel is an art medium of experiencing freedom as well as playing with color while creating painterly artworks in the process.

There is voluptuous blending with your fingers at any age with oil pastels that makes this medium unique and friendly to use.

Picasso's quote about the child artist can be experienced in old age pleasure of returning to drawing in oil pastels for a hobby or for commissions.

It is a journey different for anyone of self-discovering and self-expression through art.

You can experience oil pastel as a seasoned artist by trying this relatively new medium even if you are accomplished in watercolor or acrylics let's say.

Or you can start from scratch by buying a set of student grade oil pastels like Holbein academic only to try it out. You will be soon hooked, I assure you.

My oil pastels journey started at 53, only with my childhood and teenage exposure to art making and art readings and museums of the world visits.

I was an avid learner of several art mediums and oil pastel was my first color medium. My first art blog was called My Joy of Colors.

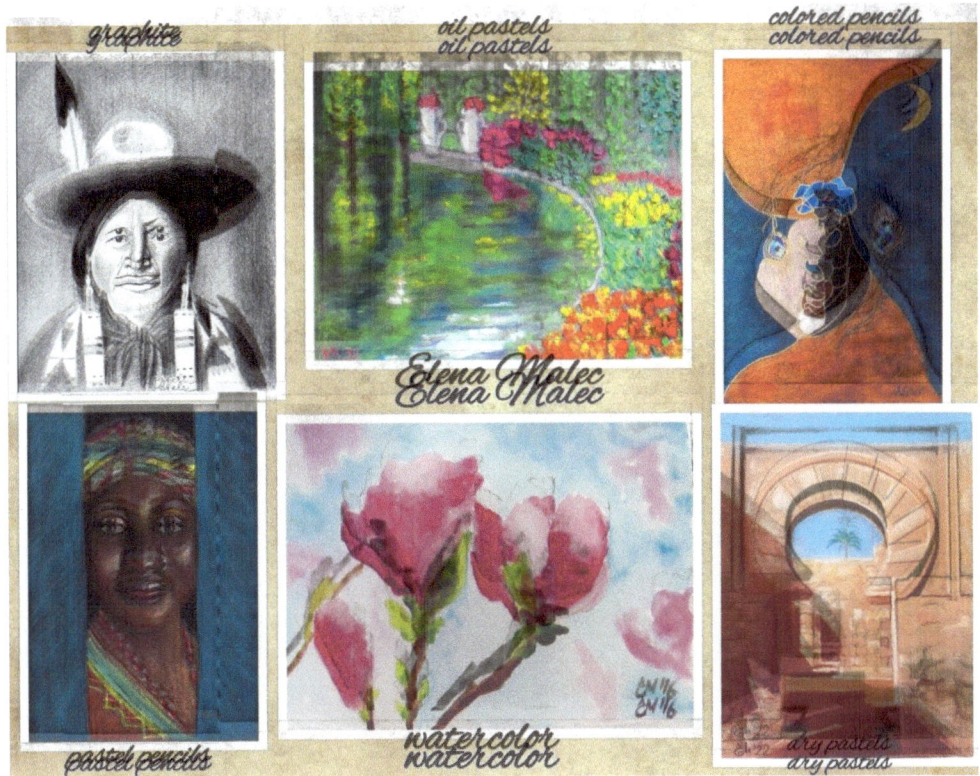

graphite

oil pastels
oil pastels

colored pencils
colored pencils

Elena Malec
Elena Malec

pastel pencils

watercolor
watercolor

dry pastels
dry pastels

Pastel Gras, Monsieur Picasso

What amazed me from the very first day with oil pastels was the versatility of the medium.

Experimenting is also part of the joy.

Rather new on the art markets oil pastels were introduced in Japanese schools for young students around 1925. Cray Pass Sakura Expressionist is till today a decent set of oil pastels to have at hand. On the professional side Holbein is the brand for artists choice.

In France, Picasso and other artists, were urging Sennelier to create a brand of portable oils and the result around 1949 was a wonderful medium that is credited to this day to the Sennelier family.

But any decent set of oil pastels is good enough to get the feeling of it and test the medium. I worked a lot with American Pentels and for apprenticeship work they do the job.

Second comes the support. Oil pastels prove their versatility in this area also. Pastel paper, sanded paper, board, cardboard, canvas, watercolor paper, glass, wood, on all of these supports they can be applied with astonishing results.

In my experiments I used cardboard, watercolor paper, pastel paper, board, canvas, sanded paper.

So how can you reach the joy of using oil pastels?

Usually applying with the stick to the support. Some artists use an underpainting in colored pencils, acrylics or watercolor. I did that too. Wonderful texture as the result.

In my pursuit of creating art, I enjoy realism and impressionism, but oil pastels can be also used in cubist or abstract styles artworks.

In this book we will delve in a few art genres suitable for oil pastels like portraiture, landscape, still life, genre paintings, and botanical.

My first 2 years of oil pastels coincide with my first 2 years of art making as an adult.

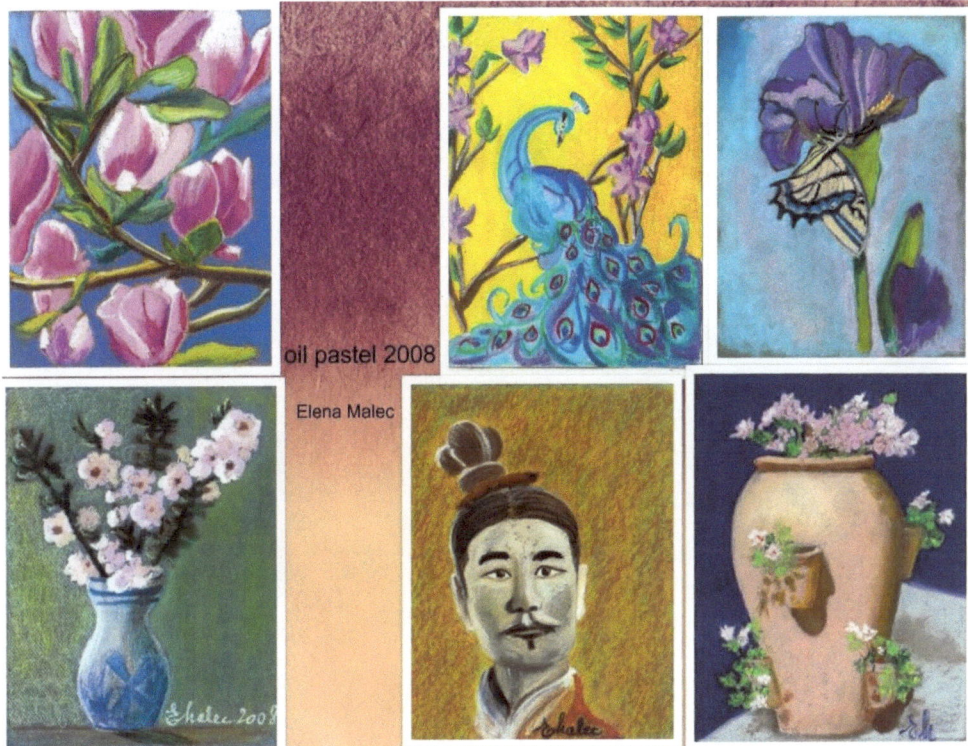

oil pastel 2008

Elena Malec

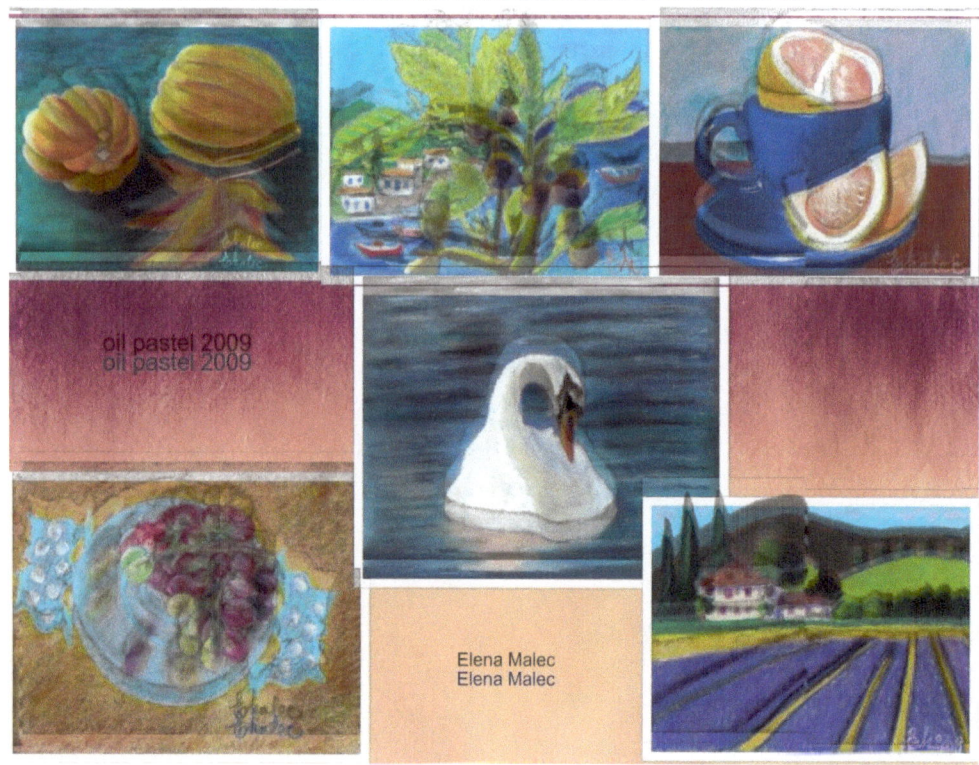

oil pastel 2009
oil pastel 2009

Elena Malec
Elena Malec

Copying the Masters

A splendid and useful exercise for the beginner artist is copying the masters. Learning by observation and study the technique of a master is good practice which makes you grow as an artist.

Any medium is right for this, from graphite to oil or less expensive oil pastels, reproductions tend to capture the unique style of a master.

You may wish to choose easy pieces or those that retain the essence of an artist style. Working with oil pastels in particular is versatile and cheap, safe, provided no solvents used.

If you are adventurous enough, you can proceed directly with oil pastels like I did with all my pieces reproduced.

Moving from one genre to another and trying out artists techniques can be a valueable experience. If your likeness with the original fails, keep working on a creative version of a piece by a master.

Good artists copy, great artists steal, used to say Picasso. After all Picasso accomplished an amazing amount of 58 paintings based on Velazquez Las Meninas.

Below my copies of some famous oil paintings, I did in oil pastel with student grade oil pastels in my first year of learning this medium and doing art in general as an adult:

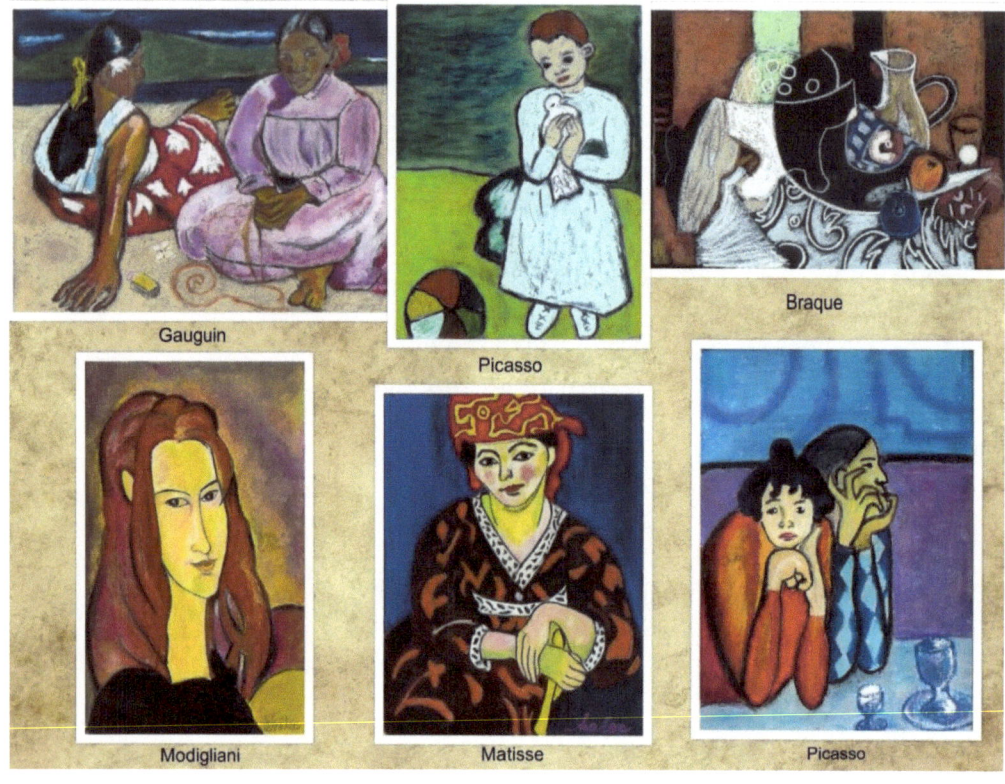

Gauguin

Picasso

Braque

Modigliani

Matisse

Picasso

This Picasso copy has an underpainting in watercolor on canvas, left.

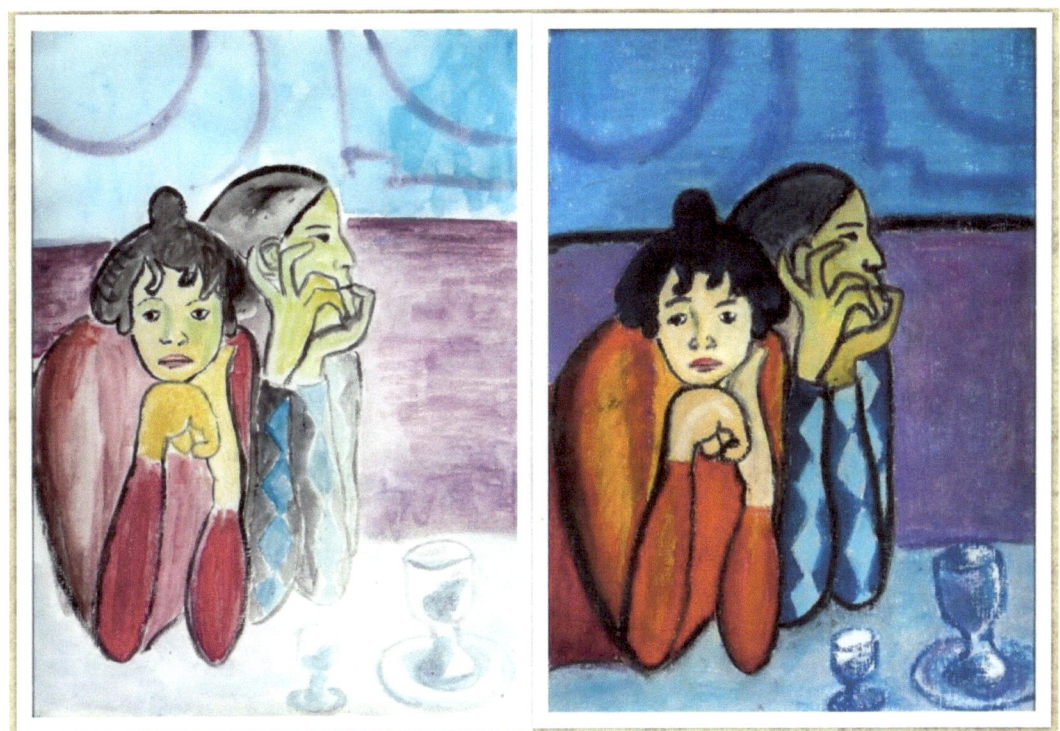

This copy has no underpainting but a simple sketch in white chalk pencil.
This copy has no underpainting but a simple sketch in white chalk pencil.

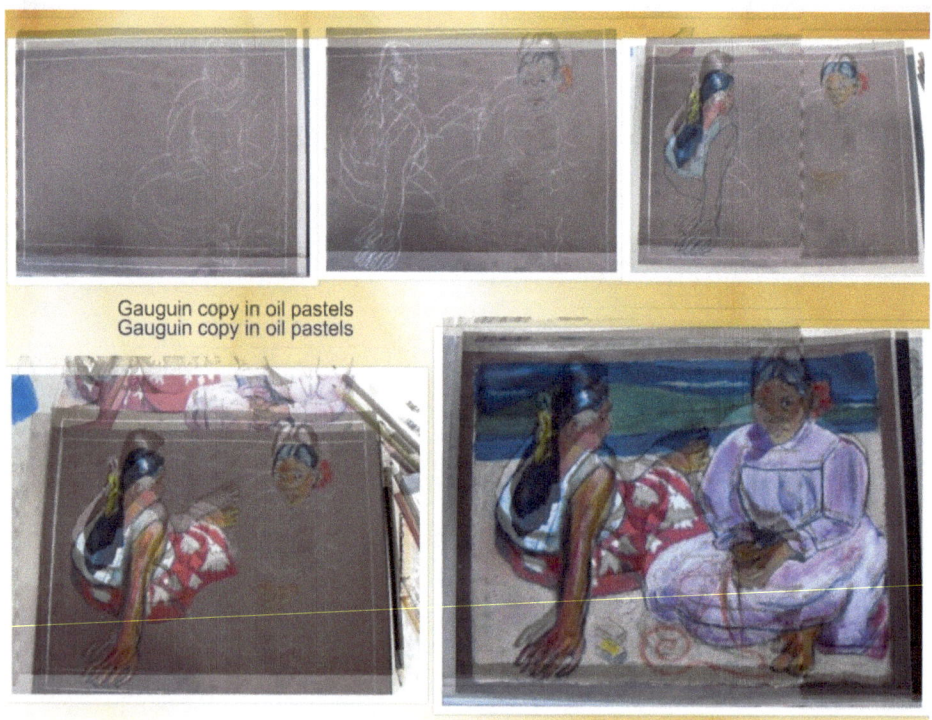

Gauguin copy in oil pastels
Gauguin copy in oil pastels

Oil Pastel Techniques

: As easy as ABC oil pastels are applied simply with the stick directly or over an underpainting.
As easy as ABC oil pastels are applied simply with the stick directly or over an underpainting.

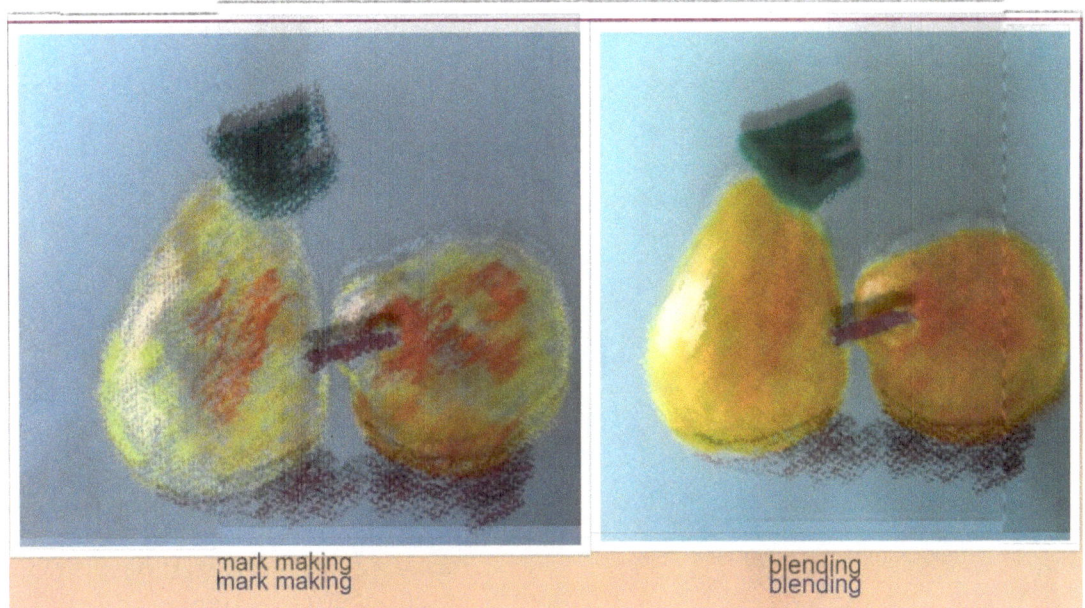

mark making

blending

Underpainting

You can have an underpainting in colored pencils, acrylics, or watercolor for your oil pastel artwork. Here, colored pencils.

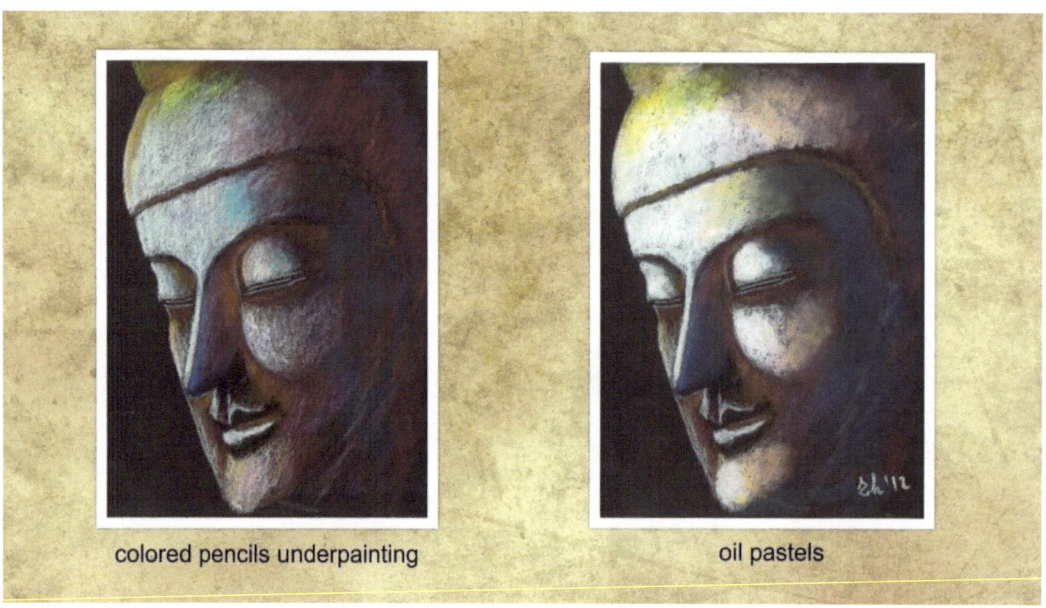

colored pencils underpainting

oil pastels

And a project on canvas.

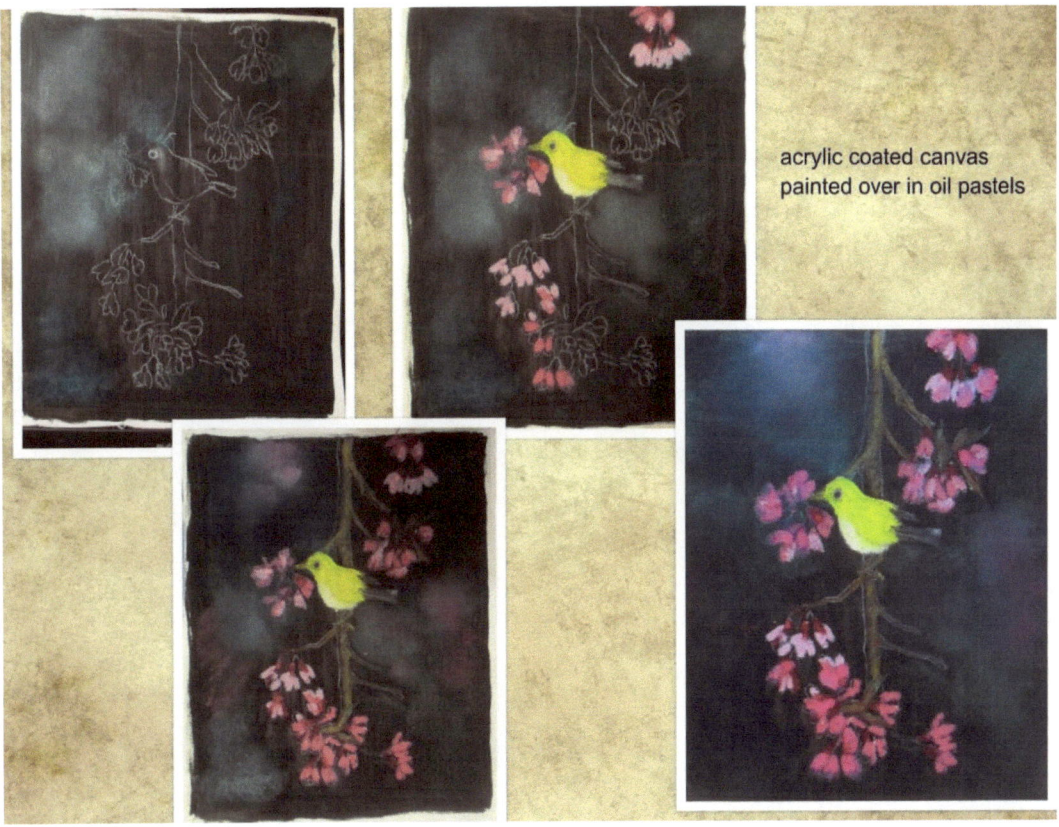

acrylic coated canvas
painted over in oil pastels

Impasto

This is a technique equally loved by oil and acrylic painters as well as oil pastel artists. It can be achieved with the stick or the palette knife usually with creamy oil pastels like Senneliers and Paul Rubens.

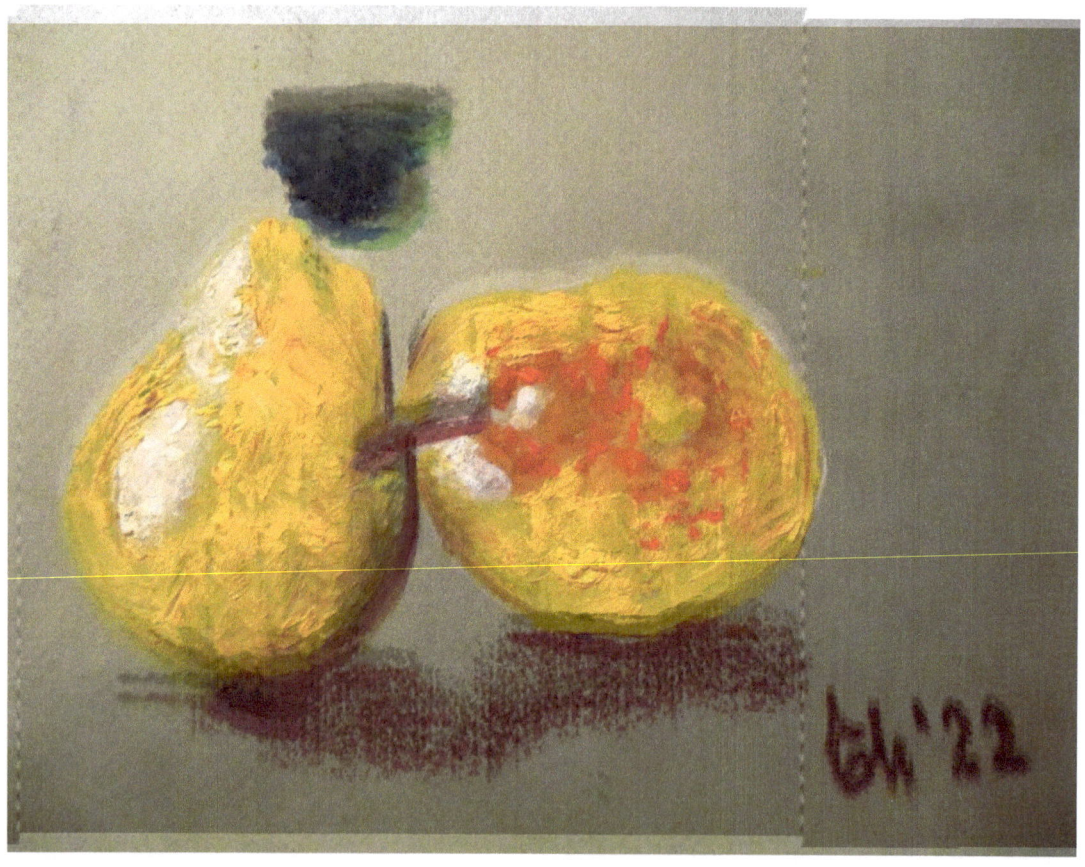

Chunks of oil pastel are amounted on the surface very crowded or superposed to create a 3D effect. No blending.

A Gandharan style Buddha from Afghanistan 300-400 AD statue in an impasto attempt after 2 years of oil pastel painting.

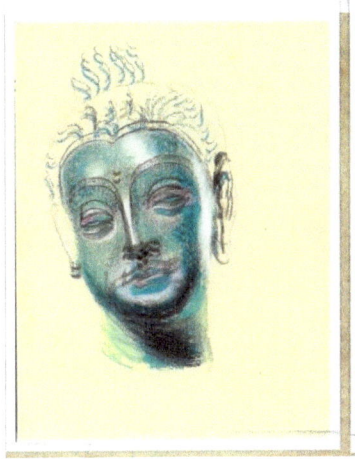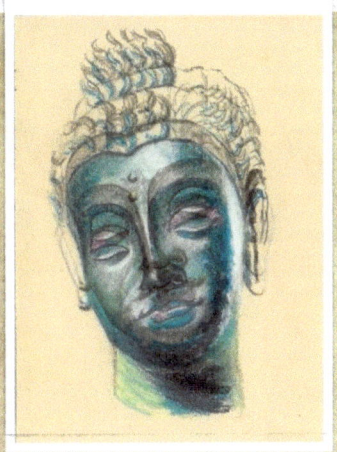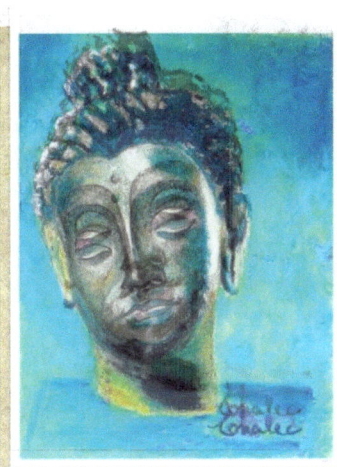

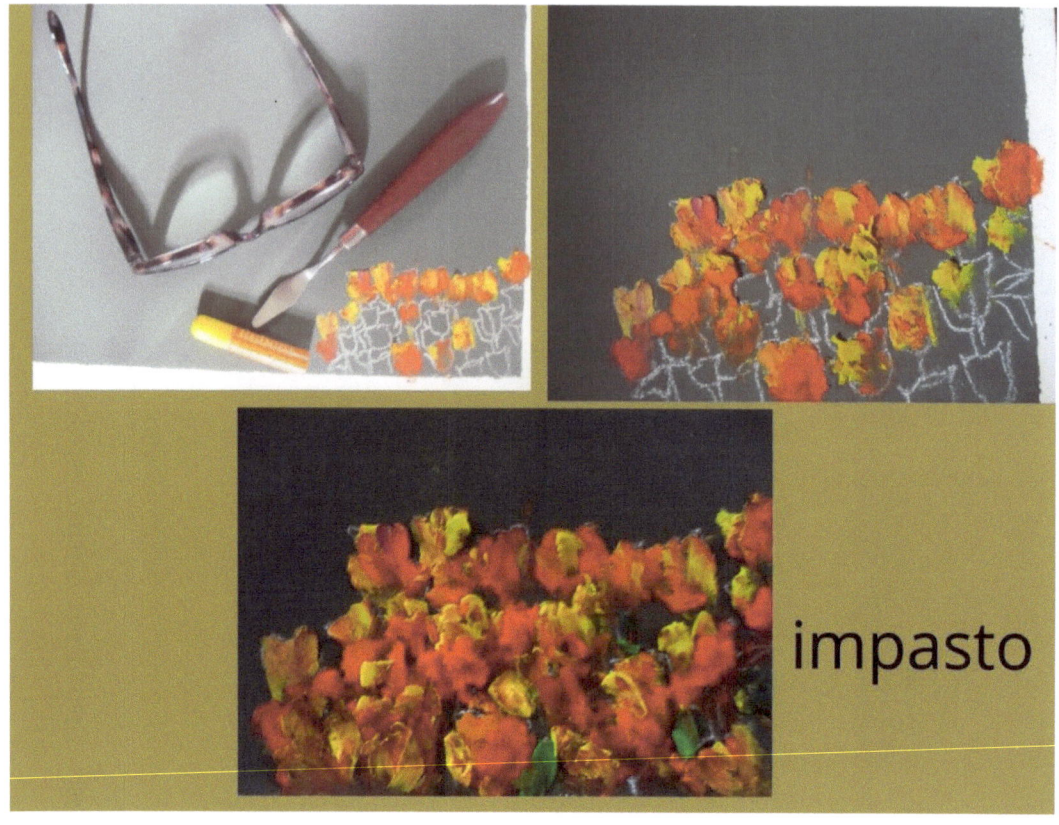

impasto

Stippling

Another way of creating effects that are rather striking and pleasant to the view, reminding of pointillism is stippling in which dots of color and pastel are layered in clusters some multicolored specks with dramatic effect.

Try with bare hand holding the pastel in a perpendicular position on the support while screwing your way into the painting.

My first attempt was on a couple of statues from a picture I took in the Museum of Asian Arts in San Francisco in 2008. I painted this statues one year later as my first year in oil pastel practice.

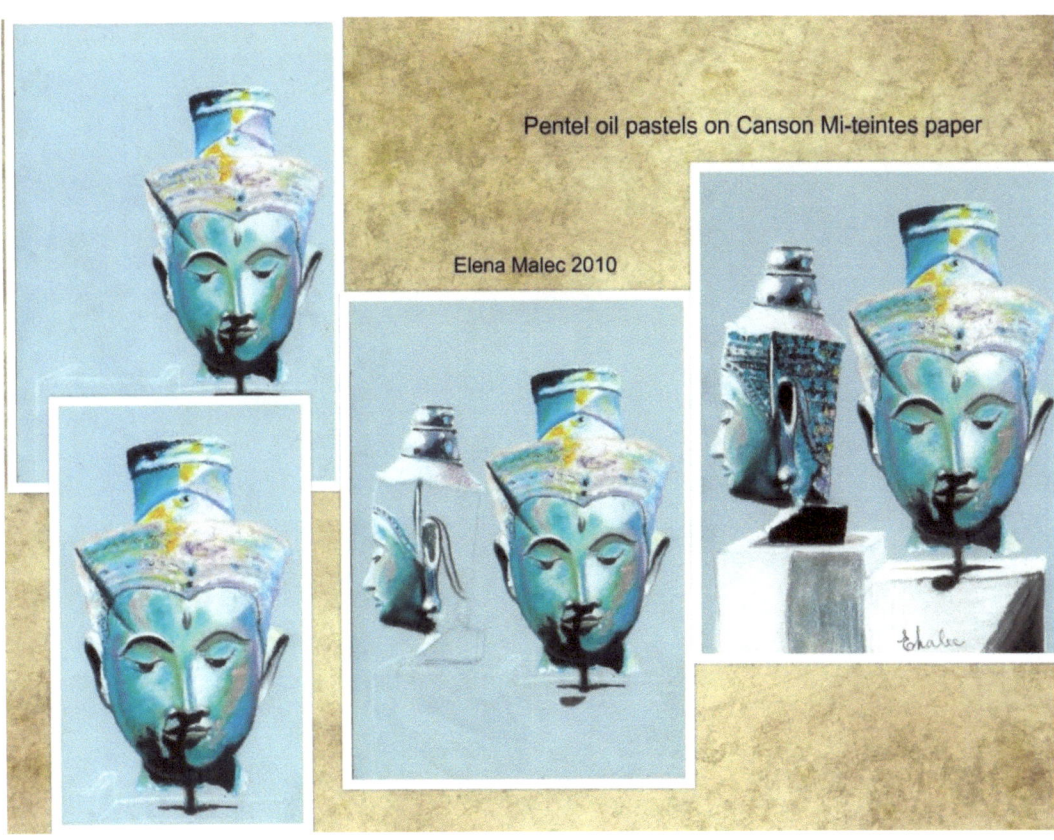

Pentel oil pastels on Canson Mi-teintes paper

Elena Malec 2010

A second version I did in 2010 with more volume as I increased the tonal values. I chose blue hues as the serene color of Buddhism.

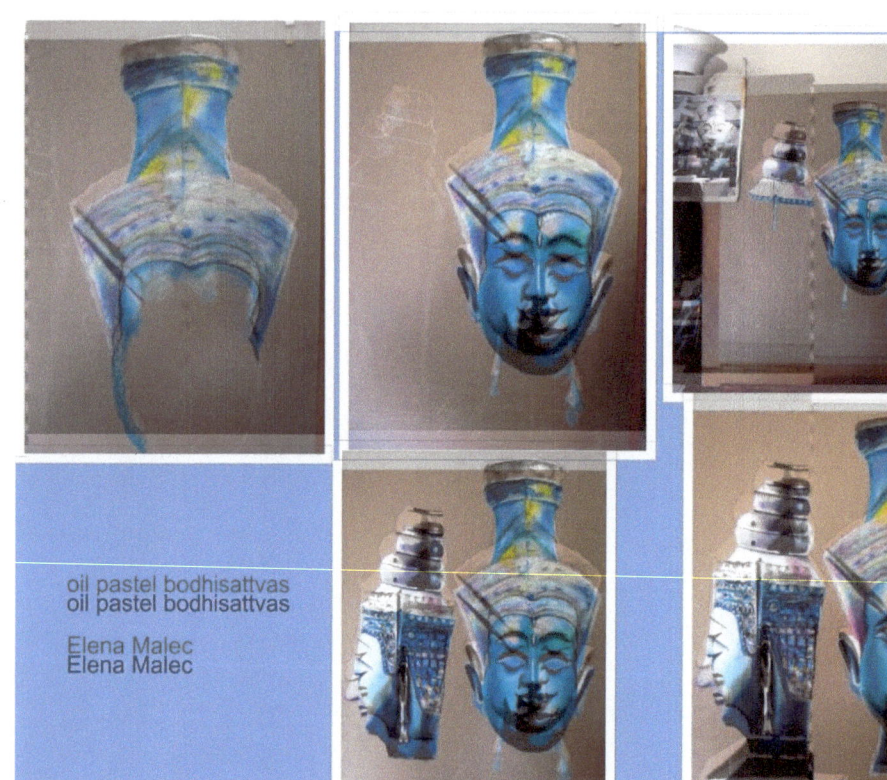

oil pastel bodhisattvas

Elena Malec

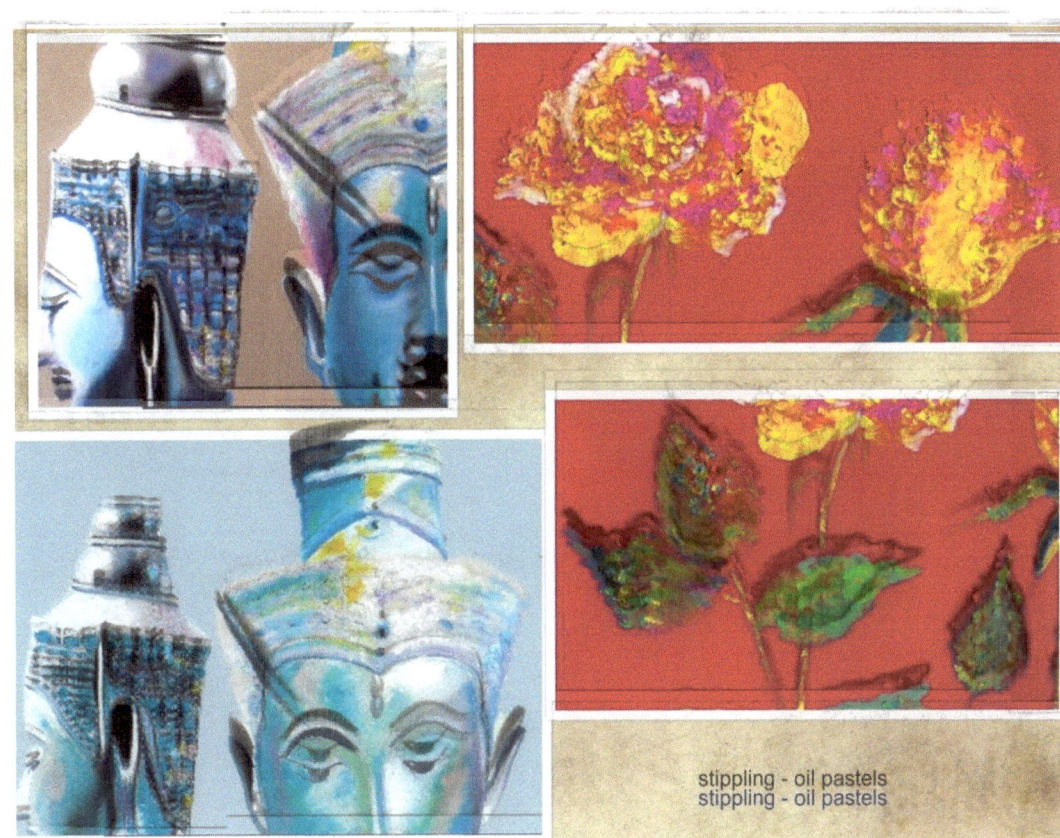

stippling - oil pastels
stippling - oil pastels

Portrait

Portrait paintings rank first in the hierarchy of art genres. An oil pastels portrait can have all the charm of oils with little fuss. Sketching from life or working from photographs can bring vividness in an oil pastels portrait alike.

One way of doing portraits when I don't work from imagination is to have a photograph from which I depart and from that point on to unleash my freedom and paint what I dream instead of what I see. The portrait can still be realistic if one sets the realistic standards to it.

There are many ways of doing portraits. From a sketch directly with the oil pastels or from a sketch in pencil you transfer on the painting surface.

Here I worked from a photograph. I first blocked in my values with a light oil pastel sketch.

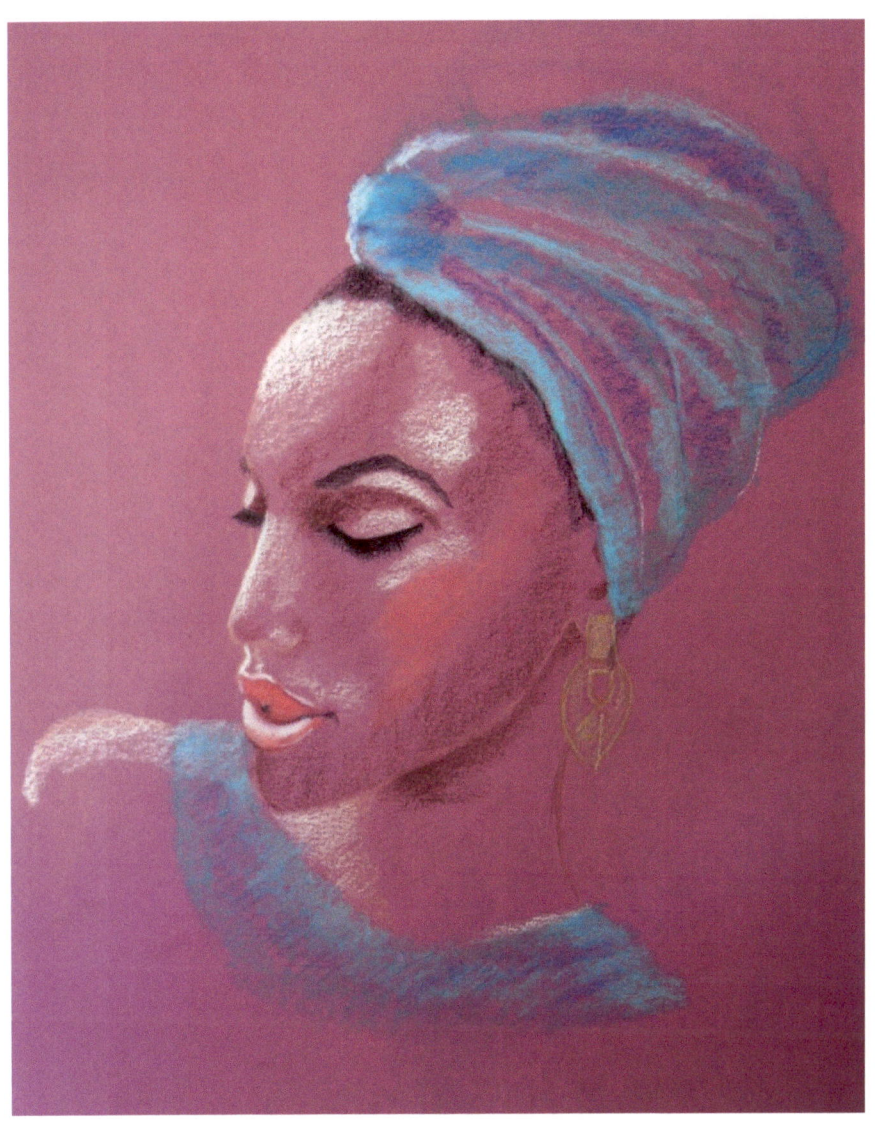

The technique used is actually blending and smudging with my finger chunks of oil pastels until I reach the smooth consistency of a dark skin. Dress and turban are done with simple hatching strokes.

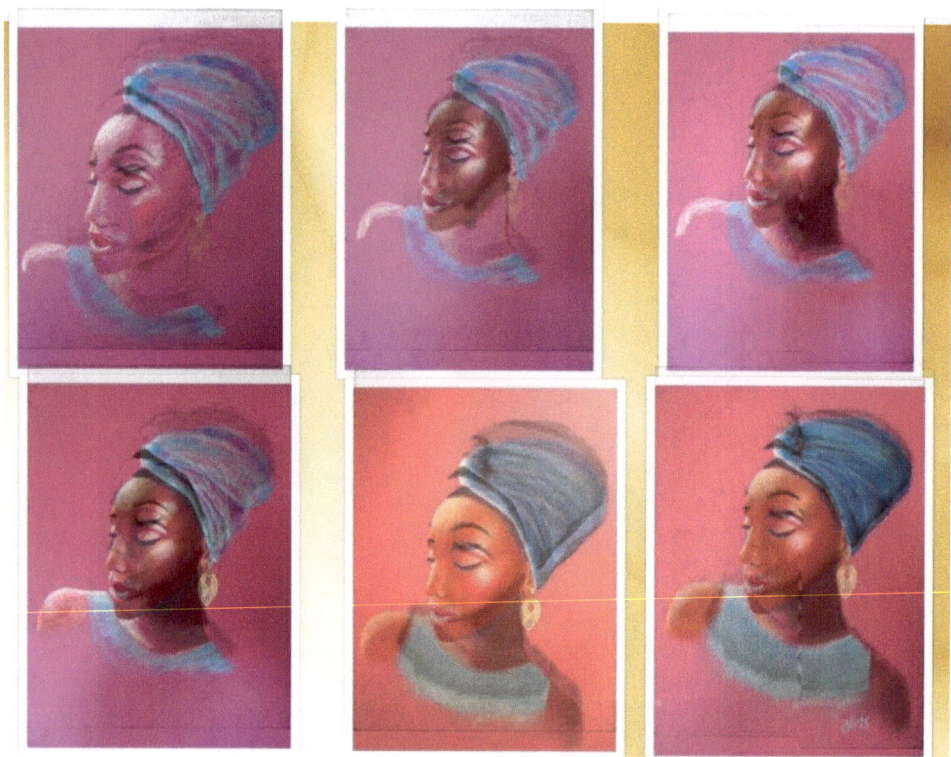

This piece measures 13x19in. oil pastel on black Canson Mi-teintes pastel paper.
This piece measures 13x19in. oil pastel on black Canson Mi-teintes pastel paper:

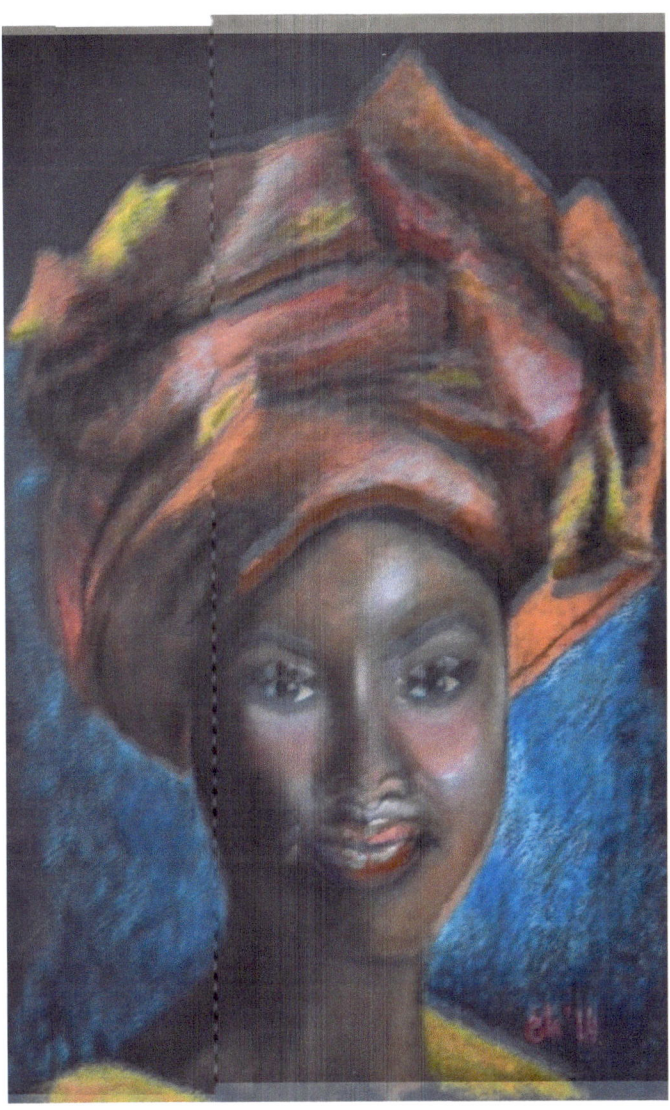

African skin tones fascinate me in oil pastels, so I have a series of African beauties done mostly while dreaming of an ideal black beauty. Here yet my composition for peace in Africa, titled An African Dream. A 9x12in. piece on black pastel paper.

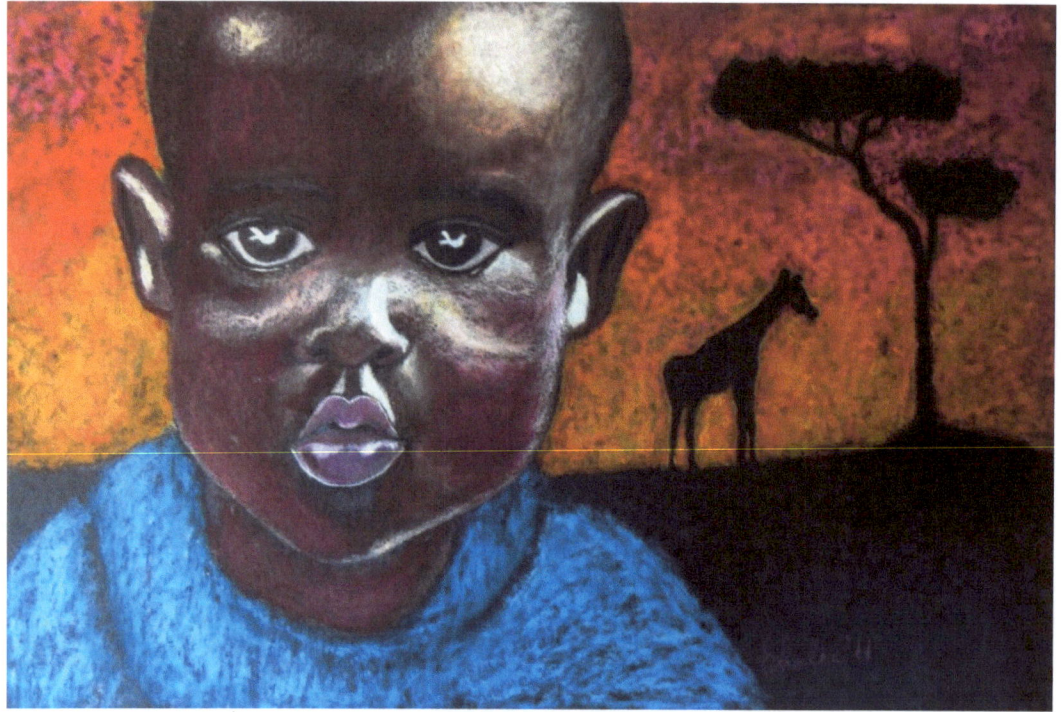

Still life

Still life subjects do not carry much prestige in fine arts being at the opposite pole to portraiture. Yet the beauty of a bowl of fruit and other inanimate objects is undeniable especially if you are fond of depicting them as I am.
I make my own still life arrangements which I paint from life or photograph and paint later. This gives me the opportunity of creating my own compositions which are never too exuberant when it comes to fruit and food items. I have a soft spot for subtle discreet still life subjects that do not overflow out of a painting. A good composition in a still life subject can have a certain amount of elements never too abundant to my taste, and as they say less is more.
Techniques vary in oil pastels from blending with the fingers to stippling and impasto with a palette knife. The last can bring the subject to life by creating an impressive 3D effect.
Supports can vary too. From canvas to paper or sanded paper anything is a good support for a still life subject that can pop up from under the glass.

This simple bowl of apples and pomegranates is achieved with a chalk sketch and blending with the finger. Occasionally I used directly the pastel stick to create texture. Sennelier oil pastels on Art Spectrum Colourfix sanded paper 9x12in.

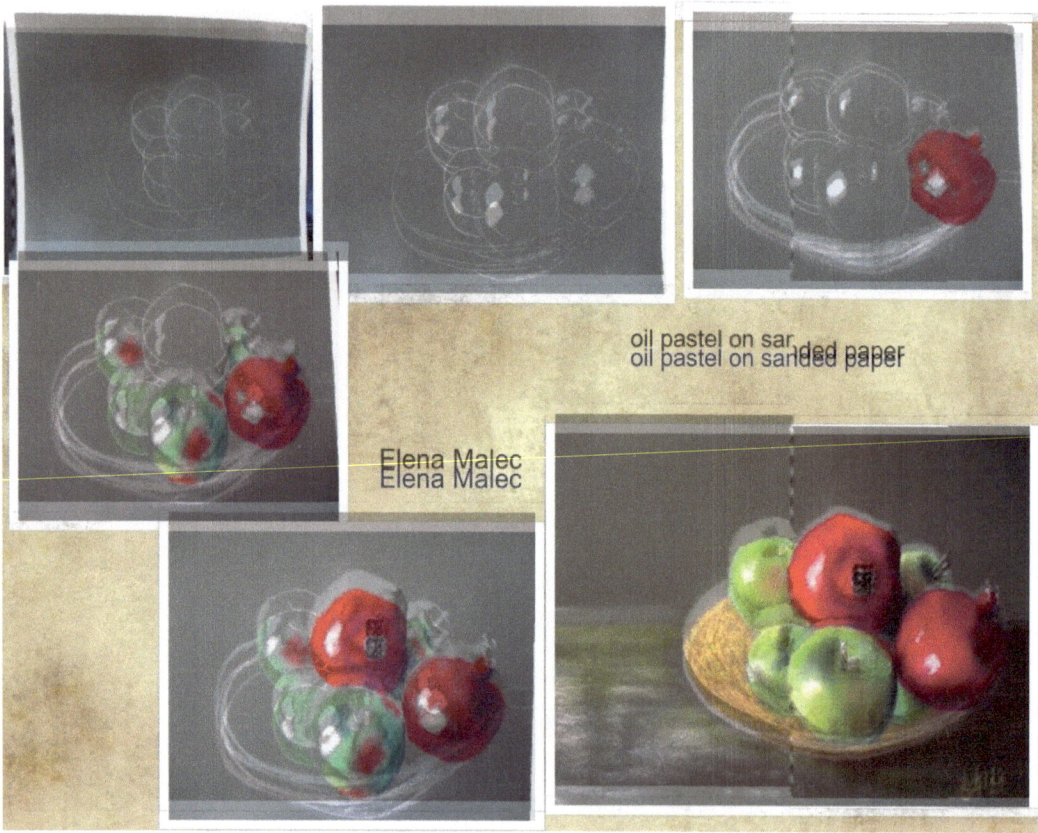

oil pastel on sanded paper

Elena Malec

Also my own composition with pomegranates on Colourfix sanded paper, 9x12i.

Also my own composition with pomegranates on Colourfix sanded paper, 9x12in.

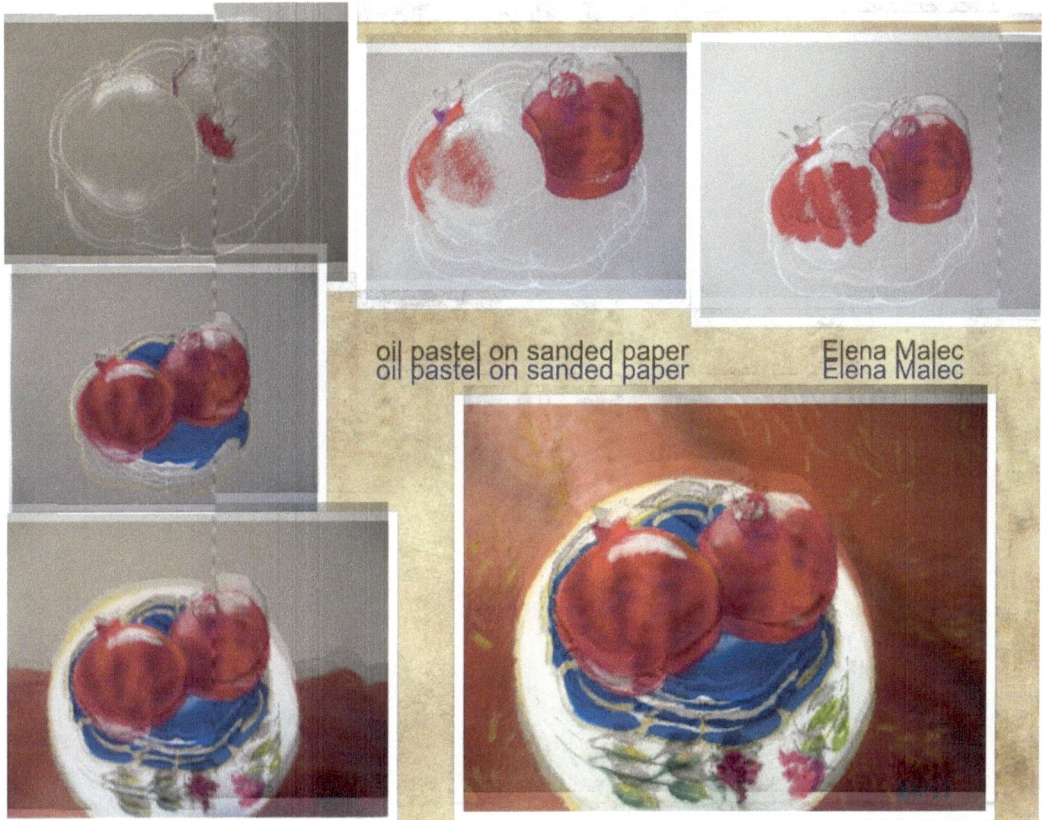

oil pastel on sanded paper   Elena Malec

Simple blending with the fingers.

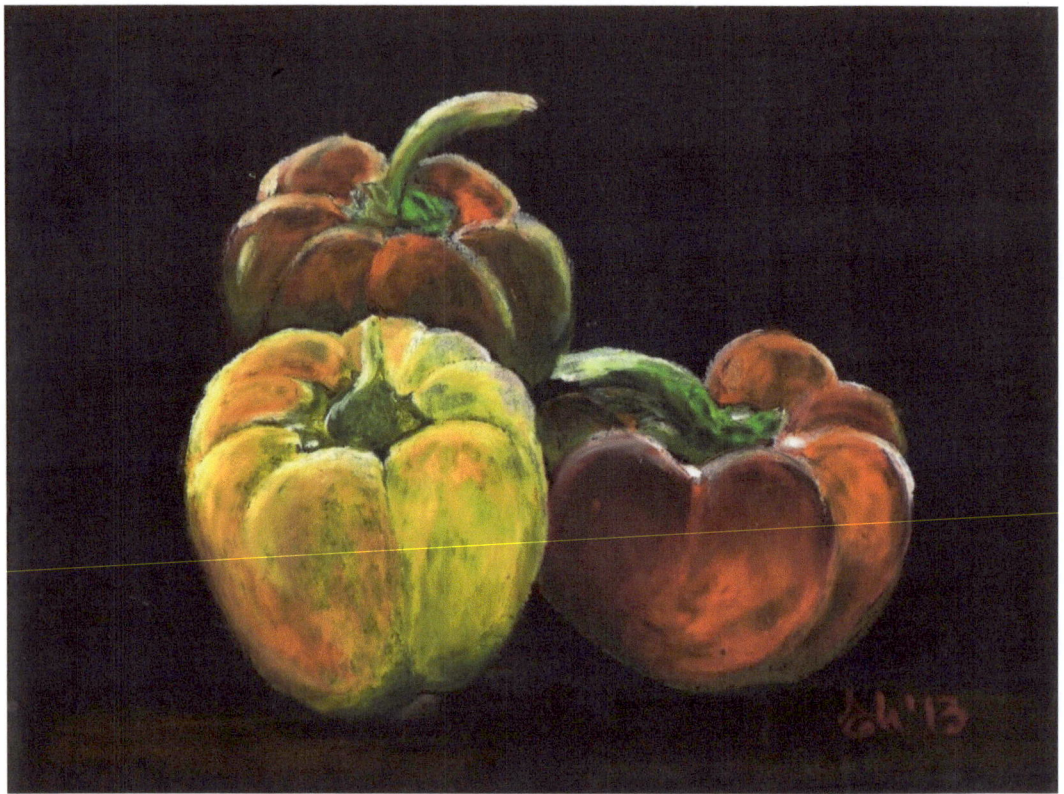

Botanical

The floral or botanical subject is considered together with still life subjects as a minor genre.
Oil pastels botanical can be very beautiful and rich in texture. Here a stippling technique for a rosebud.

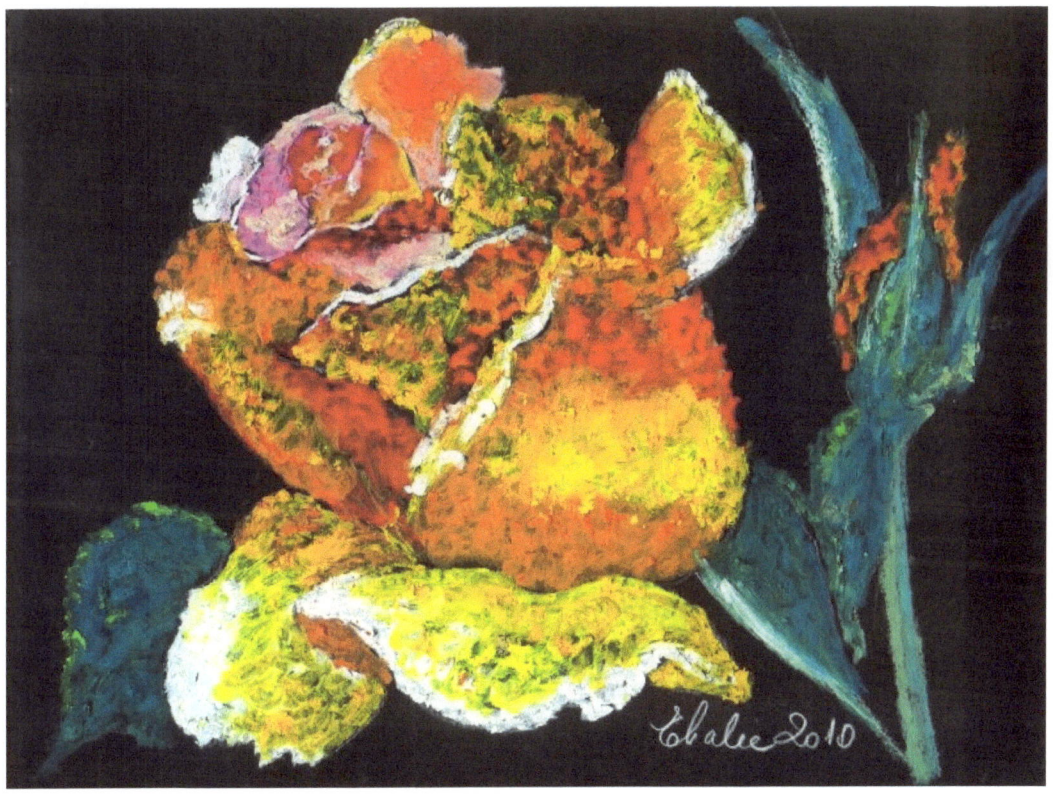

A magnolia in bloom painting I did from scratch on a 13x19in. Canson Mi-teintes pastel paper. I used as background color the blue color of the paper.

A magnolia in bloom painting I did from scratch on a 13x19in. Canson Mi-teintes pastel paper. I used as background color the blue color of the paper.

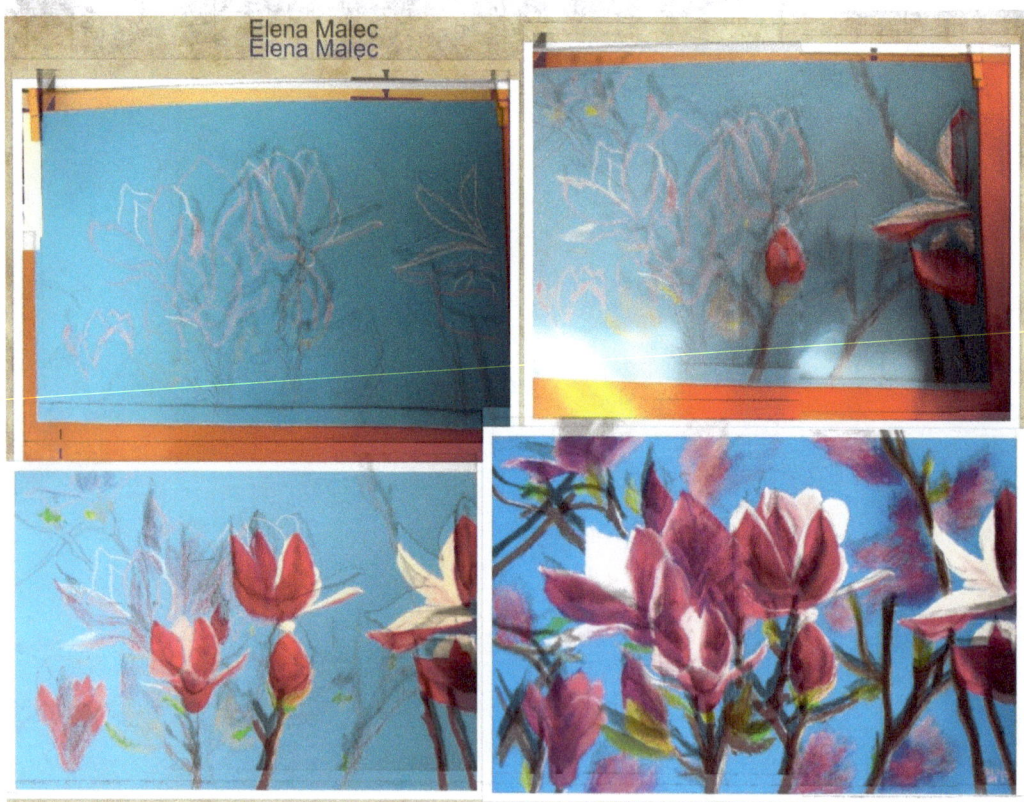

In the spring of 2017 I started a series of Ikebana morimono paintings in oil pastels after my original morimono arrangements.

In the spring of 2017 I started a series of Ikebana morimono paintings in oil pastels after my original morimono arrangements.

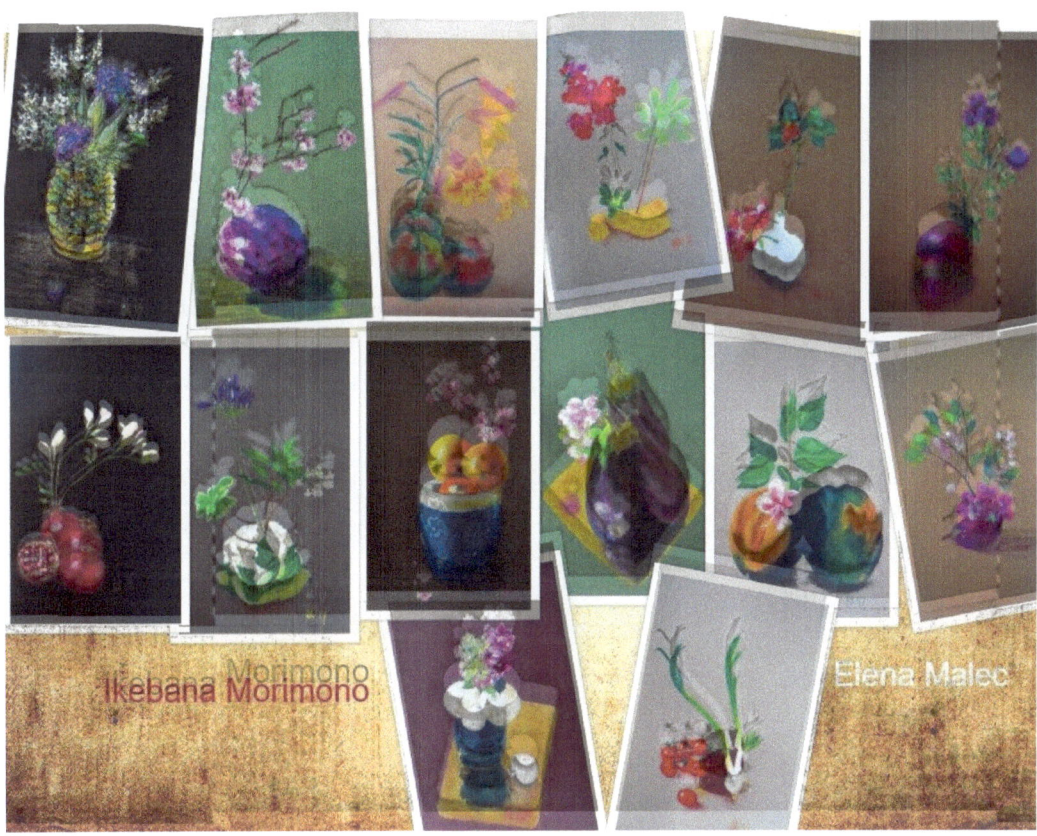

Here is the acorn squash progress.

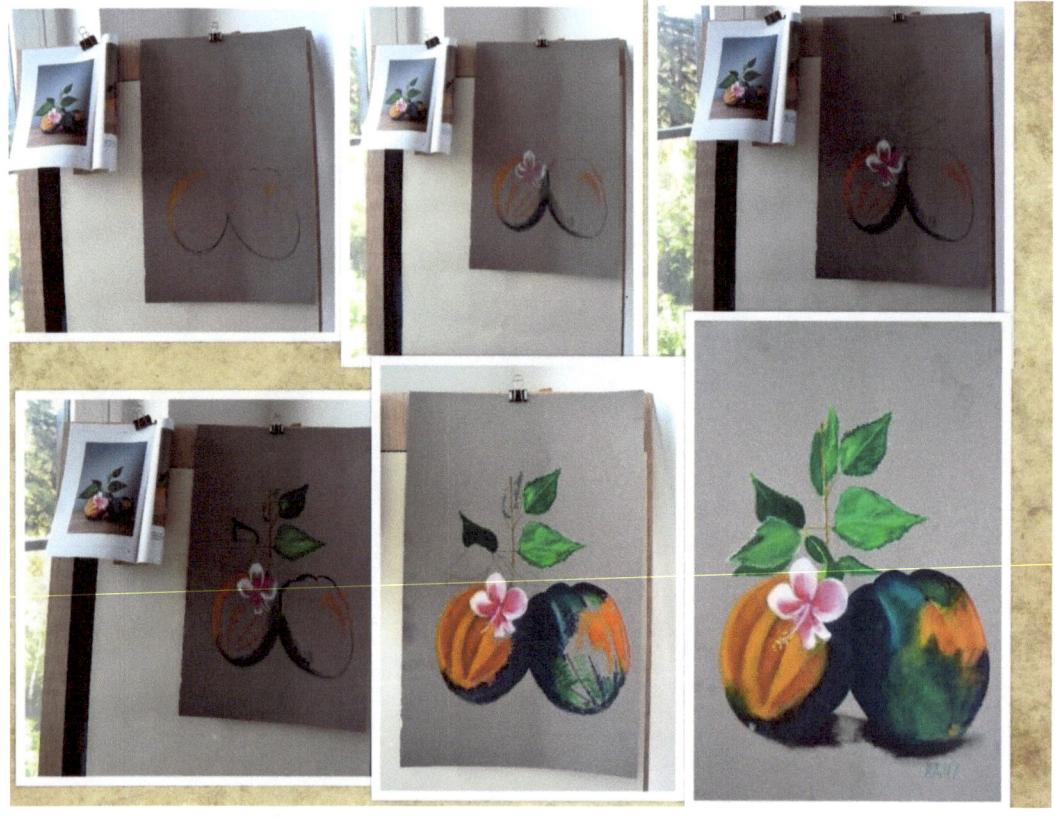

And a spring morimono in oil pastels. Morimono is a style of ikebana that translates as pile up fruit and plant material.

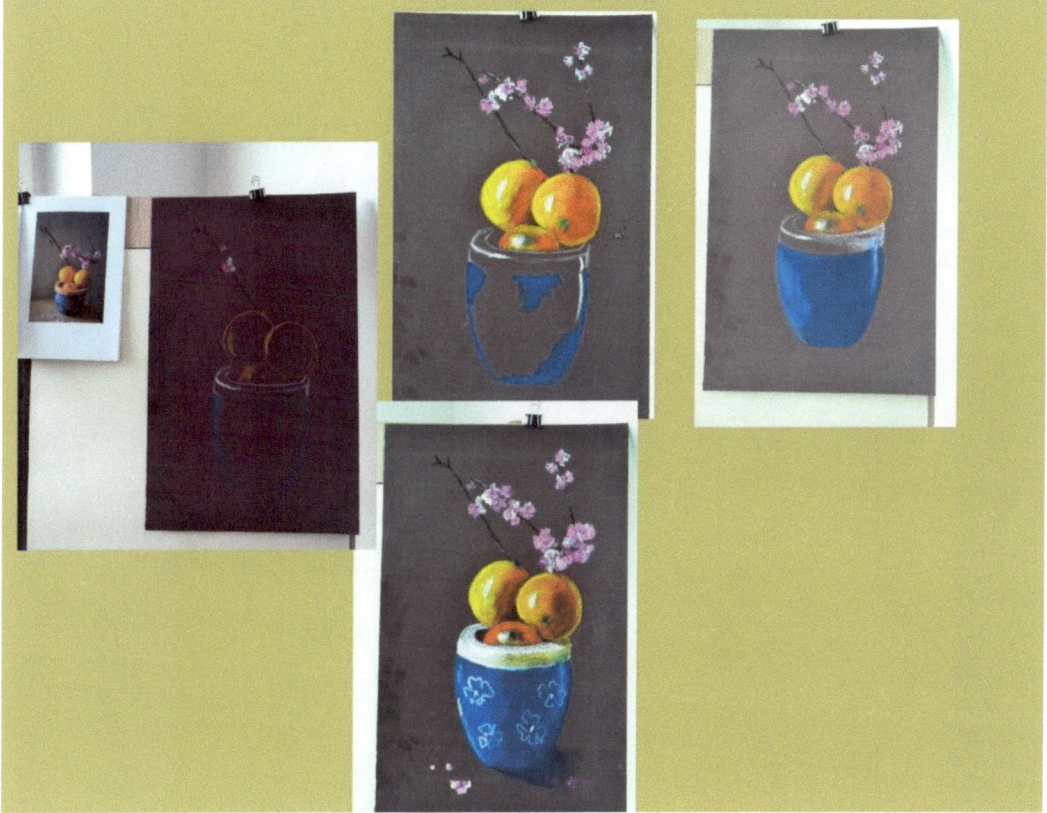

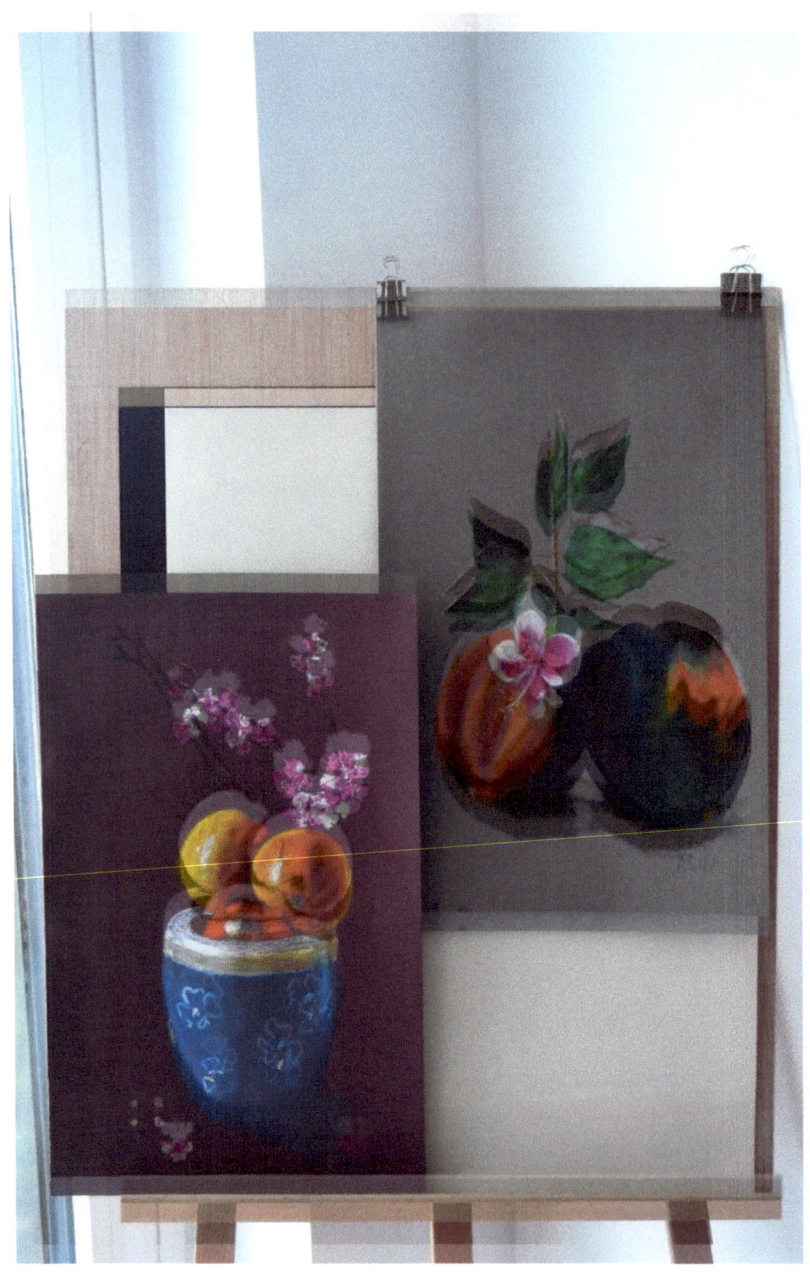

Landscape

This is a popular genre with artists and the public alike, maybe the most common when you say fine art.

There are many ways of rendering a landscape in oi pastels. One technique favored by impressionists is impasto and the beauty of this medium is that you can have vivid landscapes in impasto style in oil pastels.

Here working on a painting after my photo taken in Keukenhof botanical gardens in 2018. My photo had figures in the background which I left out and rendered only the nature subject.

For the palette knife you need patience and creamy pastels like Paul Rubens and Senneliers. But the result is rewarding. I experienced a deep calm and relaxation while painting this piece.

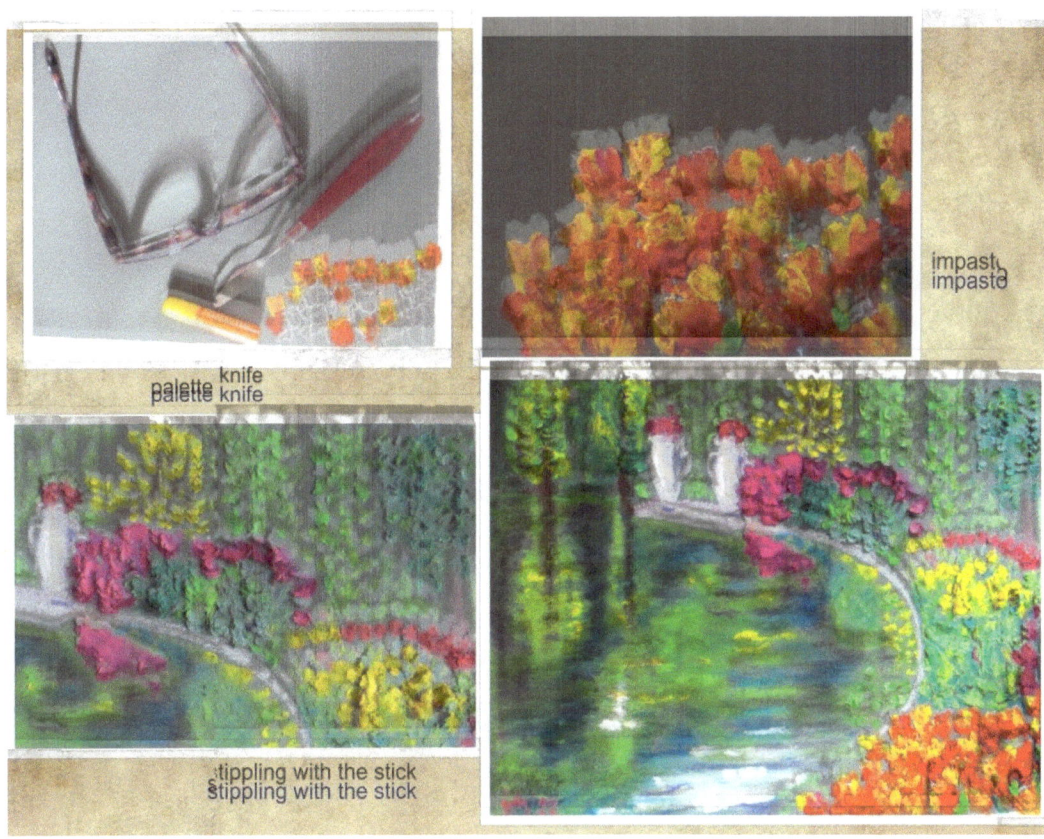

palette knife

impasto

stippling with the stick

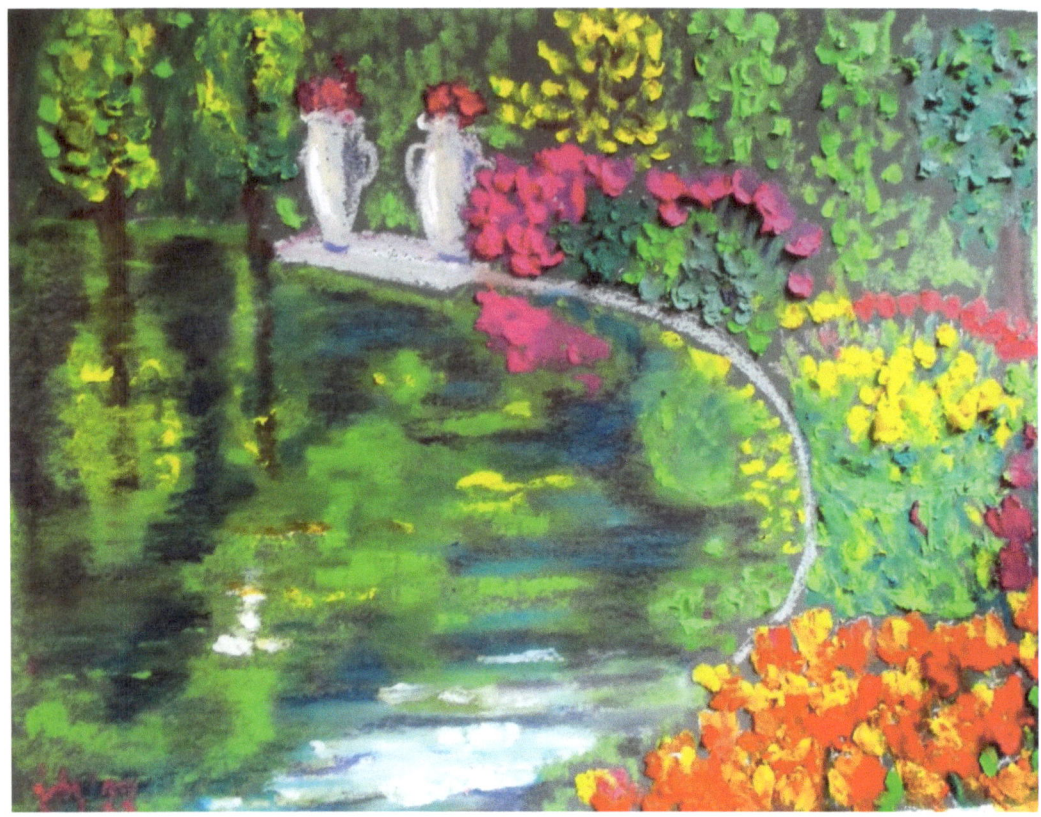

If you are an art enthusiast or hobbyist a nice way to impress your friends is to make art gifts in oil pastels after their photos.
A painting in oil pastels makes good memories last and a genuine gift at holiday time.

A vacation photo in Cordoba Spain in 2003 provided a good opportunity to paint my husband pictured from the back while walking in the narrow streets of this fascinating city. The challenge of this pastel was to draw the urban perspective and also is the figure drawing.
I did a sketch in graphite pencils, then using tracing paper transferred to the support which was Canson Mi-teintes 9x12in. From there on the painting took its normal course.
Here you have a city scape, I kept it simple, no details as I wanted to focus on the urban appeal of this medieval European city.

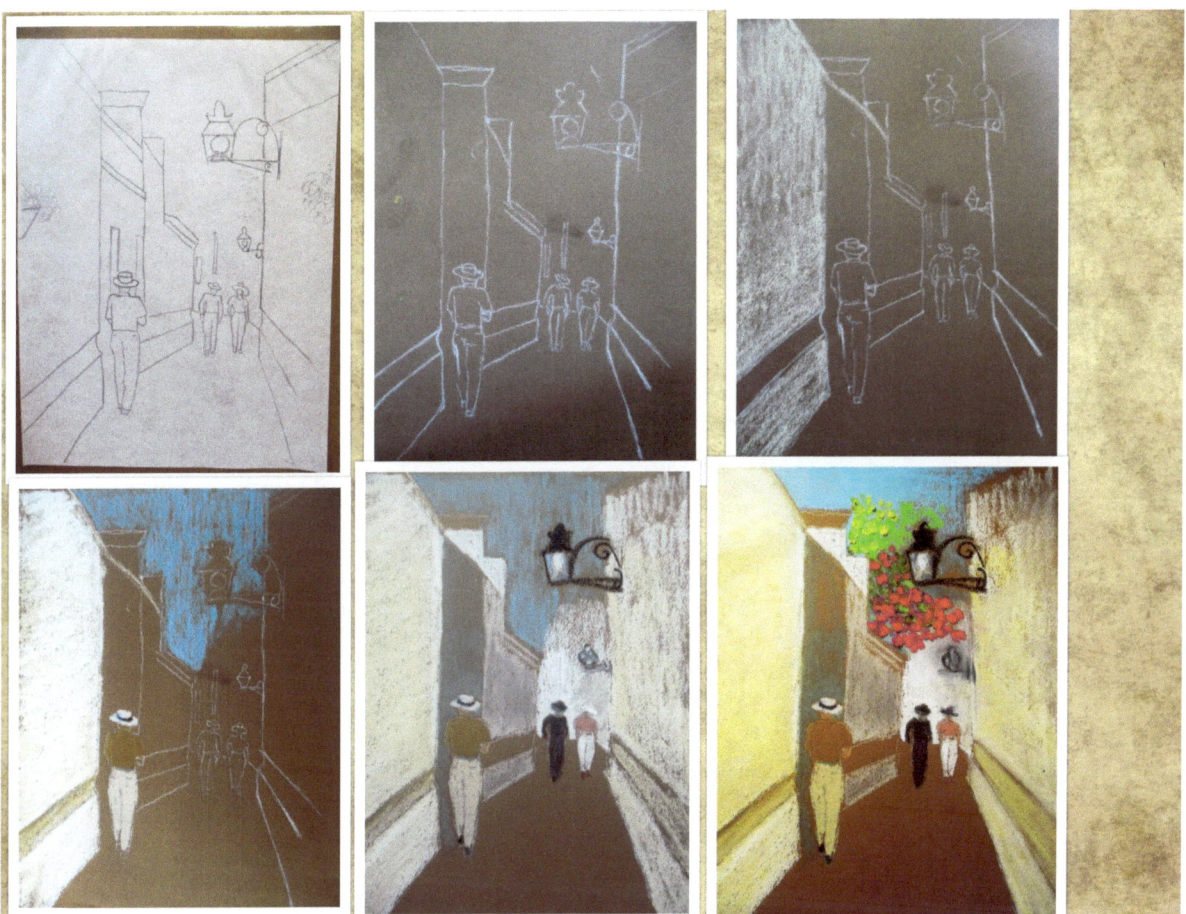

„Sombrero cordobes", Sennelier oil pastels on 9x12in. Canson mi-teintes paper.
„Sombrero cordobes", Sennelier oil pastels on 9x12in. Canson mi-teintes paper.

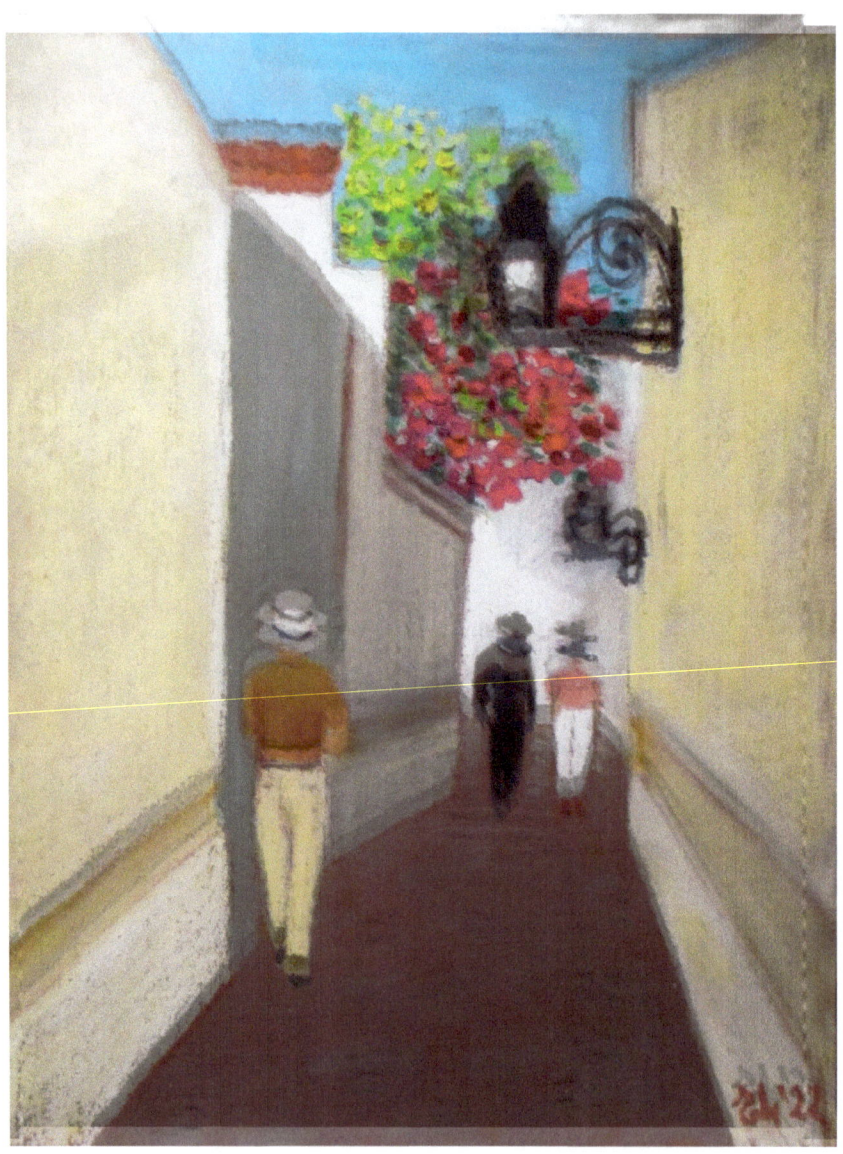

Genre paintings

Travel photos can be a trove of inspirational subjects for your oil pastels. While in China we attended a Peking Opera performance. This is a 9x12in. Sennelier oil pastels on sanded paper.

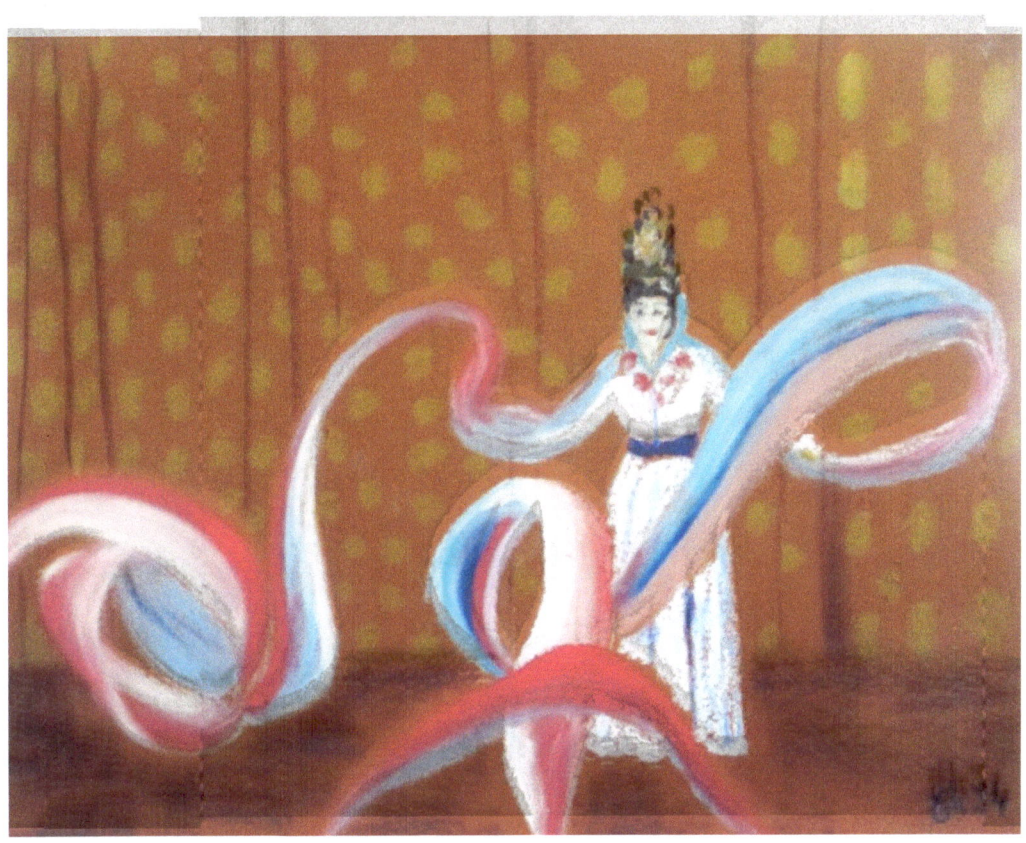

Self-portrait

Self-portraits can be realistic, impressionist, with likeness or without. Any artist draws several self-portraits along his career. My self-portrait with Turkmen takhya, 9x12in. Sandpaper.

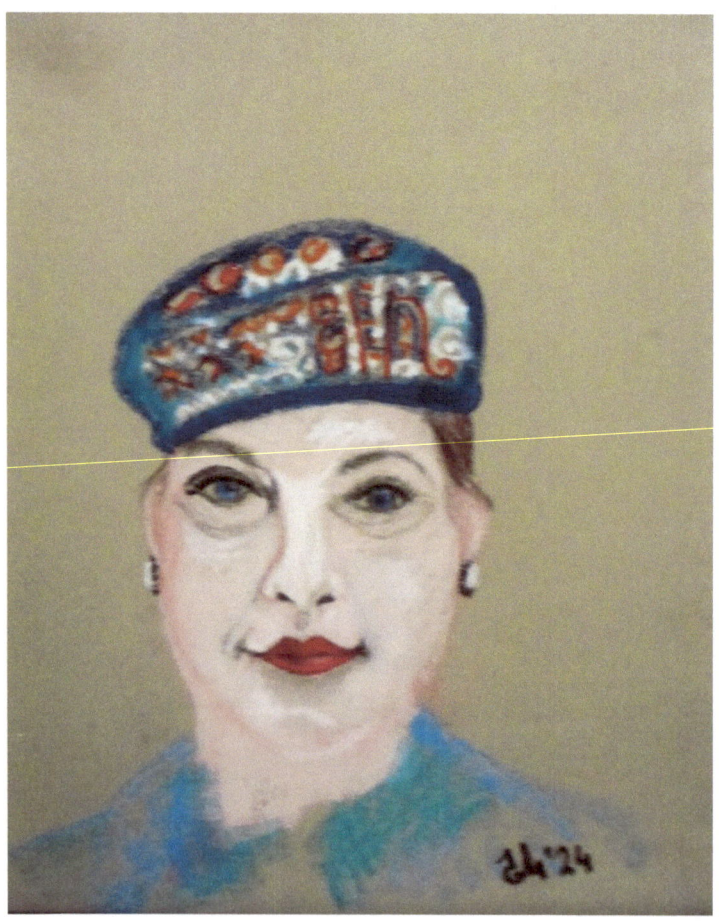

Afterword

This book about my oil pastel journey came to an end but my journey continues, your journey possibly will begin after reading my adventure with the medium. Maybe you already started playing with oil pastels and hoped as I do to find more about them in my experience and experiments.

Please remember to enjoy every moment of making art.

Buy yourself some good tools and make that painting you dream about.

And don't forget to protect your finished work under glass always even when it is on stretched canvas.

Sketch everyday in your sketchbook. Train your eye in aesthetic ways. Plan virtual or physical visits to fine art museums.

Take good photos, create your own compositions and arrangements. Remember that a good painting starts with a perfect composition. And a composition is about unity, color, balance, about light and shadow, about point of interest, about a positive message.

Spread the word. Join oil pastels artist communities, take part in weekly or monthly challenges, create your own challenges. Only this way you can grow as an artist.

Art is about setting one free. I never felt so free before making art. I never felt the beauty and joy of colors before oil pastels.

Never stop to wonder at nature's work and create artworks full of wonder.

www.ingramcontent.com/pod-product-compliance
Lightning Source LLC
Chambersburg PA
CBHW051949210526
45474CB00003B/71